PUFFI

Family Phantoms

Gervase Phinn is a teacher, freelance lecturer, author, poet, educational consultant, school inspector, visiting professor of education and, last but by no means least, father of four. Most of his time is spent in schools with teachers and children.

He has written two hugely successful books for adults, *The Other Side of the Dale* and *Over Hill and Dale*, two volumes of children's poetry, and he is currently finishing his first novel for children.

Books by Gervase Phinn

For children

FAMILY PHANTOMS

THE DAY MY TEACHER WENT BATTY
IT TAKES ONE TO KNOW ONE

For adults

THE OTHER SIDE OF THE DALE
OVER HILL AND DALE

Gervase Phinn

Family
Phantoms

Illustrated by Chris Mould

PUFFIN

PUFFIN BOOKS

Published by the Penguin Group
Penguin Books Ltd, 80 Strand, London WC2R 0RL, England
Penguin Putnam Inc., 375 Hudson Street, New York, New York 10014, USA
Penguin Books Australia Ltd, 250 Camberwell Road, Camberwell, Victoria 3124, Australia
Penguin Books Canada Ltd, 10 Alcorn Avenue, Toronto, Ontario, Canada M4V 3B2
Penguin Books India (P) Ltd, 11 Community Centre, Panchsheel Park, New Delhi – 110 017, India
Penguin Books (NZ) Ltd, Cnr Rosedale and Airborne Roads, Albany, Auckland, New Zealand
Penguin Books (South Africa) (Pty) Ltd, 24 Sturdee Avenue, Rosebank 2196, South Africa

Penguin Books Ltd, Registered Offices: 80 Strand, London WC2R 0RL, England

www.penguin.com

First published 2003
1

Text copyright © Gervase Phinn, 2003
Illustrations copyright © Chris Mould, 2003
All rights reserved

The moral right of the author and illustrator has been asserted

Set in 12/16 Joanna

Made and printed in England by Clays Ltd, St Ives plc

British Library Cataloguing in Publication Data
A CIP catalogue record for this book is available from the British Library

ISBN 0–141–31446–X

To my children, Richard, Matthew, Dominic and Elizabeth

Contents

Phamily Phantoms

My father is a *Werewolf*,
My mother is a *Witch*.
My Auntie May's a *Vampire*,
And lives inside a crypt.
My Uncle Stan's a *Goblin*
My Auntie Jean's a *Ghoul*
My cousin Tom's a little *Imp*
Never goes to school.
My sister Pat's new husband
Is the *Phantom of the Manor*,
He comes to life at midnight,
And hits you with a spanner.
Our Maureen is a *Poltergeist*,
And so's my brother Bob,
Who recently got married
To the *Creature from the Bog*.
My grandad is a *Zombie*,
Who haunts the church at night,
Dressed only in his underwear,
He's not a pretty sight.
My grandma is an ancient *Spook*,
The daughter of a *Sprite*,
She roams around the neighbourhood,
When you've turned out the light.
Uncle Paddy is a *Leprechaun*,
Furry, fat and frisky,

He lives in a distillery,
And samples all the whiskey.
Our Brenda is a *Banshee*,
And our Gary is a *Gremlin*,
Trevor is a hairy *Troll*,
But we don't talk about him.
It's strange that with these relatives,
I'm as normal as can be,
But it's magic on a Sunday,
When they all come round for tea.

Why?

Why do the white sails shiver?
What is that shaking on deck?
Why do the tall masts tremble?
Don't you know? It's a nervous wreck!

The Nokk

Be warned, you little children,
Every son and every daughter,
Don't disobey your mums and dads,
And play too close to water.

For in every roaring river,
In lake and pool and lock,
In waterfalls steep and chasms deep,
There lurks the deadly Nokk.

His beard is of a weedy green,
His ears like giant oars,
His eyes are the hue of the ocean blue,
And his hands are giant claws.

He sits and waits in his watery cave,
And never makes a noise,
Or silently swims near the surface clear,
Looking for girls and boys.

And should he spy a child like you,
Playing near waters deep,
With his click-clack jaws and his snip-snap claws,
He'll grab you by the feet.

Then he'll drag you down to his murky depths,
To the watery world of the fish,
And on his rock, the deadly Nokk,
Will eat his tasty dish.

So be warned, you little children,
And obey your parents, do.
Every son, every daughter, stay away from the water,
Or his next meal might be YOU!

Yeti

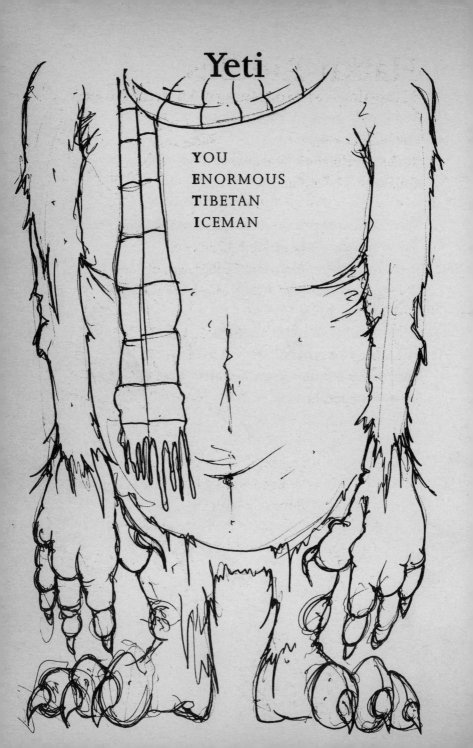

YOU
ENORMOUS
TIBETAN
ICEMAN

Haiku Riddles
Mythological Monsters of Ancient Greece

She posed a riddle
Which if you could not answer,
Gulp! She ate you up.

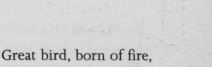

Great bird, born of fire,
Feathers like flickering flames,
Eyes which burnt like coals.

Hair, a nest of snakes,
Eyes that could turn you to stone.
Look not upon her.

Lightning carrier,
Winged white horse of the muses,
Born of a Gorgon.

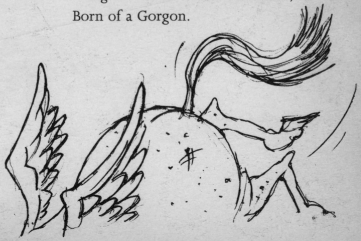

Nymphs of the ocean,
Who charmed the passing sailors
With their soft voices.

Greedy, gobbling birds,
Shrieking like the angry wind,
Feathers hard as iron.

Bull-headed monster,
Which dwelt in the Labyrinth,
Deep below the earth.

Three-headed watchdog,
Who guarded the gates of Hell.
Beware his sharp teeth.

Solutions on page 103

The Lament of Frankenstein's Monster

I'm made up of odd bits and pieces,
That the young Baron cobbled together.
My hair is long, black and spiky
And my skin is the colour of leather.
My ears are of different sizes,
And so are my arms and my legs,
And my eyes are of different colours,
From my neck sprout two bolt-like pegs.
I'm a giant of mammoth proportions,
A freak with a horrible face,
But one thing you can be quite sure of –
My heart is in the right place.

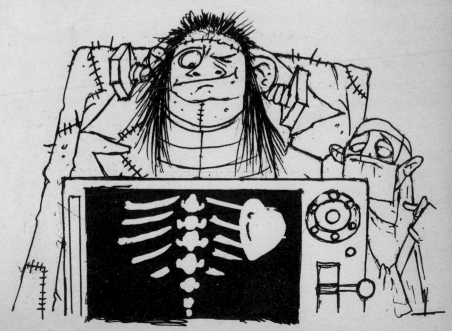

The Frog Prince

On a giant lily pad,
A lonely bullfrog sat.
He croaked and croaked from morn 'til dusk
Round and green and fat.
Then one day a princess came,
And spied him sitting there.
Her skin it was as soft as silk,
And flaxen was her hair.
The frog he leapt into the pond,
He swam with all his might,
And jumped on to a rotting log,
His golden eyes so bright.
'Oh, princess fair, I am your prince,
Oh, kiss me quick,' he cried.
'Are you the one I'm searching for?'
'My prince,' the princess sighed.
Then reaching out into the pond,
She stroked his slimy head.
'Oh kiss me! Kiss me!' cried the frog,
'And soon we shall be wed.'
The princess smiled a little smile,
Then plucked him from the log.
'I think I'd rather have,' she said,
'A little talking frog.'

The Little Devil

'Mummy, Mummy, can you tell me
Why our baby's hair's so black?
Why it shines like raven's feathers
And grows in bunches down his back?
And Mummy, Mummy, can you tell me
Why his eyes are big and bright,
And why his teeth are long and pointed,
And flash like daggers in the light?
Mummy, Mummy, can you tell me
Why he has such long sharp nails
And why his little feet are cloven?
Do all young babes have pointed tails?
Mummy, Mummy, can you tell me
Why there're horns upon his head
And why smoke bellows from his nostrils,
And why his skin's the brightest red?'

'Of course, I know the reason, darling,'
Replied the mummy to the lad.
'He looks the way he does, my angel,
Because he takes after his dad!'

After Hours

There were:

    Lions roaring,
    Wolves howling,
    Pigs snoring,
    Tigers growling,
    Crows cawing,
    Wild cats prowling.

There were:

    Bull frogs burping
    Black bats squeaking,
    Great slugs slurping,
    Eagles screeching,
    Crickets chirping,
    Zoo door creaking.

But:
    As the keeper peered inside,
    He smiled, he nodded, then he sighed.

For: You could have heard a pin drop!

The Unicorn

Before the rivers and the seas,
Before the meadows and the trees,
Before the sunset and the dawn,
The unicorn was born.

With silver mane and coat of white
And hooves as black as the blackest night,
With gentle eyes and twisted horn,
The unicorn was born.

The Loch Ness Monster

When the dancing shadows darken,
O'er the heather on the brae,
When the pale moon shines and shivers,
'Neath a sky of silvery grey,
When the whispering wind is silent,
At the closing of the day,
Something stirs deep in the water,
In the weeds below the bay.
Now is the time when all are sleeping,
The Loch Ness Monster comes out to play.

Swimming, sliding,
Slithering, gliding,
Leaping, lunging,
Bubbling, plunging,
Coiling, curving,
Spiralling, swerving,
Diving, dipping,
Arching, slipping,
Floating, twirling,
Twisting, curling.
Hear him calling in the gloom,
See him basking 'neath the moon.

14

But when the dancing shadows vanish,
O'er the heather on the brae,
When the bright sun gently rises,
Casting far its golden rays,
When the whistling wind starts blowing,
At the dawning of the day,
Something dives deep in the water,
To the weeds below the bay.
Now is the time when all are waking,
The Loch Ness Monster hides away.

No more swimming,
No more sliding,
No more slithering,
No more gliding,
No more leaping,
No more lunging,
No more bubbling,
No more plunging,
No more coiling,
No more curving,
No more spiralling,
No more swerving,
No more diving,
No more dipping,
No more arching,
No more slipping,
No more floating,
No more twirling,
No more twisting,
No more curling.
There is a silence in the air.
The creature is no longer there.

Now 'til night the monster sleeps,
Where it's cold and dark and deep,
Waiting for the close of day,
When he'll again come out to play.

Poltergeist

There's a poltergeist in our house,
He's as quiet as a mouse!
But he appears at the dead of night,
Just when I've turned out the light . . .

    And tramples on the flowers,
    And breaks the greenhouse windows,
    And leaves the gate open,
    And lets my hamster out,
    And drops sweet papers,
    And turns the lights on,
    And takes biscuits,
    And leaves the fridge open,
    And breaks my sister's toys,
    And leaves my bike out in the rain,
    And hides my slippers,
    And leaves dirty washing everywhere,
    And messes up my room,

    And lots of other things besides.

But my dad does not believe in ghosts!

Letter to the Headteacher

Dear Sir,

I'm writing this letter to tell you
Why our Jason is away.
He looked so pale and poorly
When he got home yesterday.
His face became quite hairy
And his teeth grew sharp and white,
His ears got long and pointed,
And he looked a sorry sight.
Then his eyes became quite bloodshot
And his nose all wet and black,
And claws grew on his fingers,
And bristles sprouted up his back.
The doctor when he saw him,
He had a nasty fright.
In all his years of medicine,
He's never seen the like.
Of course, it was unwise of him
To recommend the vet –
Our Jason's very sensitive,
He's not a household pet!
But I can understand the doctor,
Running quickly from the room,

When Jason started howling,
And pointing at the moon,
And slavering and growling,
And trying to bite his throat,
He hadn't time to open his bag,
And write a doctor's note.
You'll understand, I'm certain,
Why our Jason is away
He looked so pale and poorly
When he got home yesterday.

Mrs W. Wolfe

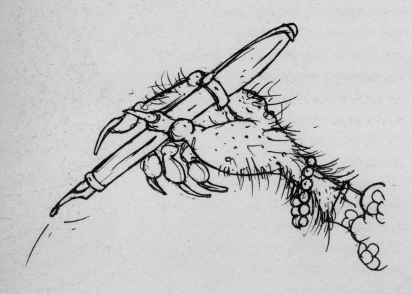

The Wizard

On the black rocks by the bay,
A tower rises gaunt and grey.
It is the home, so people say,
Of the Wizard of the West.

The castle walls are sheer and high,
Its turrets touch the very sky,
And every window's like an eye
Of some great towering beast.

And in that fort of gaunt grey stone
The wizard sits there all alone,
And glowers from his granite throne
And dreams of dreadful deeds.

A tangled mane grows from his head,
Above grey eyes as dull as lead,
Around the mouth — a slit of red —
And a hard and hook-like nose.

His beard is long and snowy white,
His cloak is blacker than the night,
Spangled with stars, which catch the light,
And golden mystic shapes.

With silver wand he weaves his spell,
And chants the charms he knows so well,
A magic he will never tell,
To any living soul.

Hocus-pocus, magic potions,
Mumbo-jumbo, good-luck lotions,
With his wand he waves and motions,
Around his bubbling pot.

He turns a fly into a frog,
Transforms a spider to a dog,
Summons up a swirling fog,
Or whistles up the wind.

With magic belt and lucky stone,
Moonstone ring and wishing bone,
The wizard conjures all alone
In his gaunt grey tower.

When all the fields are swathed in snow,
And round the wall the cold winds blow,
And the moonlight casts an eerie glow,
You'll hear him in his tower.

On the black rocks by the bay,
A tower rises gaunt and grey,
It is the home, so people say,
Of the Wizard of the West.

A Matter of Fact

Who is that howling outside the door?
No one — it's just the wind's wild roar.

Who is that tapping on the window pane?
No one — it's just the driving rain.

Whose is that cold and deathly face?
No one's — it's just the fireplace.

Whose is that long and skeletal hand?
No one's — it's just the umbrella stand.

Who is that visitor in the hall?
No one — it's just shadows on the wall.

Who is that figure on the stair?
No one — there is nothing there.

Whose are those eyes which shine so bright?
No one's — it's just the candlelight.

Is that a phantom form I see?
No, no, my friend, it's only me.

Such sights and sounds fill me with dread,
And ghostly thoughts rush through my head.

Such strange imaginings you should resist,
There's no one there — I do insist.
As a matter of fact — I don't exist!

The Nuckelavee

'Have I told you bairns the story?'
Asked Grannie Mac one day,
'Of great great Uncle Alec,
And what happened on the brae,
When he was out a-walking
At the closing of the day?
Och! I must have told you that wee tale.

Your great great Uncle Alec
Was the strongest and the best.
Why, even in midwinter
He wouldna wear his vest,
And he could play the Scottish pipes
Much better than the rest.
Och! I must have told you that wee tale.

Well, one December evening,
It was dark and dismal weather,
When Uncle Alec donned his coat
And brogues of finest leather,
And went in search of his stranded sheep,
Amidst the snow and heather.
Och! I must have told you that wee tale.

To keep him company in the cold,
His bagpipes he did play,
And the sad and lonely music
Echoed soft across the brae,
Like a distant choir of angels,
You might hear on Judgement Day.
Och! I must have told you that wee tale.

The west wind blew, the sky turned black
And in the moon's pale light,
The rocks took on the shape of beasts
In a sea of ghostly white,
And great great Uncle Alec
Wished he was at home that night.
Och! I must have told you that wee tale.

But still he played his bagpipes
As he stood there all alone.
Then he heard a sort of snuffling
And a sniffling and a groan,
And a grunting and a howling
And a long and lingering moan.
Och! I must have told you that wee tale.

In the silvery moonlight
A creature then appeared,
With great red jaws and coal black claws
And a tangle of a beard,
And with its large and bloodshot eyes
At Uncle Alec peered.
Och! I must have told you that wee tale.

Its body was a barrel shape,
Its arms were long and thin,
Its yellow veins pulsated
'Neath the cold, translucent skin,
And as Uncle Alec stood there
The creature breathed on him.
Och! I must have told you that wee tale.

Its monstrous head rolled wildly,
And the crimson jaws gaped wide
And it glared in ghoulish pleasure
At the victim by its side,
And on that bare and barren brae
Your uncle couldna hide.
Och! I must have told you that wee tale.

Now every true born Scotsman knows
From Glen Garry to the Dee
About this dreadful creature,
'Tis called the Nuckelavee,
And should it clasp you in its claws,
You'll end up as its tea.
Och! I must have told you that wee tale.

And every true born Scotsman knows,
From Loch Lomond to the Tay,
To escape the creature's clutches
There is only one sure way,
And that is to make music
And on the bagpipes play.
Och! I must have told you that wee tale.

So your uncle played upon his pipes
A melancholy strain,
And when it heard the mournful tune
The creature turned quite tame,
And its large red eyes they filled with tears
And it shook its snow white mane ...
But it ate poor Uncle Alec,
For its supper just the same.
Och! I must have told you that wee tale.'

The Redundant Vampire

I come from a long line of vampires,
My blood line stretches way back
To the castle in old Transylvania
To the time of good old Count Drac.
I am one of his noble descendants
The very last one in the crypt
And my coffin is battered and dusty
And my cloak is old and ripped.
Oh, but I was a wonderful vampire,
I had charm, sharp teeth and good taste.
Now I can't even get in my coffin
I've varicose veins and a forty-inch waist.
I remember when I was a youngster,
My hair was as black as the night.

Now I'm bald and the hair that I have got
Has turned the whitest of white.
My eyes were as red as great rubies
And they'd dazzle the victims I'd meet.
Now I have to wear glasses for reading
And I can't see beyond twenty feet.
My fangs were fierce and full-blooded,
They were sharp, they were long, they were white,
Now they sit in a glass at my bedside
And they don't give a very good bite.

How I long for the days of my childhood,
When I was a strip of a lad,
When I chased all the bats round the belfry
And had a pint with my great Uncle Vlad.
In those days the people were frightened,
They'd run screaming when I came in sight.
Now they look and they laugh and make faces
And it's me who is given the fright.
Yes, I come from a long line of vampires,
And I am the last in the line.
Life with old Dracula was truly spectacular.
I'm long in the tooth and that is the truth,
There's far too much room in this draughty old tomb,
I'm anaemic and cold and lonely and old.
I'll go into a coma without a blood donor.
I'm a real nervous wreck and a pain in the neck,
And I don't have a very nice time.

An Irish Fairy Story

'As I was walking home one night,
When the air was still and the stars shone bright,
I saw as plain as plain can be,
A leprechaun beneath a tree.
His coat was of a shamrock hue,
His stockings red, his britches blue.
With tiny shoe upon his lap,
The fairy cobbler tap, tap, tapped.

I thought, "If I could catch that sprite,
As he tap, tap, tapped in the moon's pale light,
If I could that wee fairy hold,
He'd take me to his crock of gold."
And so across the grass I crept
And from behind the tree I leapt.
I grasped the coat of shamrock hue,
As he tap, tap, tapped on his weeny shoe.

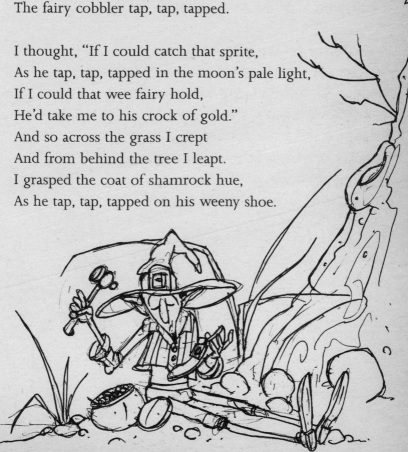

"Your crock of gold!" I loudly cried,
"I haven't one," the fairy lied.
Then in a twinkling of an eye
He disappeared and that's no lie,
And in his place appeared this bird,
A pheasant fat, upon my word.
And as I held it on my lap
I felt on my shoulder a tap, tap, tap.'

'Now let me get this story right,
You were walking home in the moon's pale light
When you claim that underneath this tree
A fairy cobbler you did see.
For forty years as a judge I've sat
And I've never heard the likes of that,
And much as I like your fairy tale,
The poaching's proved, so off to gaol!'

Limerick

My cousin, an explorer called Betty,
Grew fat eating plates of spaghetti.
On a trek in Tibet,
She was caught in a net
And displayed in the zoo as a Yeti.

Monster Alphabet 1

A is for **ALIEN** arriving by air,

B is for **BASILISK** with the deadliest stare,

C is for **CYCLOPS**, he's only one eye,

D is for **DRAGON**, he'll light up the sky,

E is for **EXTRATERRESTRIAL CREATURES**,

F is for **FRANKENSTEIN** of the frightening features,

G is for **GRIFFON**, a lion with a beak,

H is for **HYDRA**, the many-headed freak,

I is for the **INVISIBLE SPIRITS** of night,

J is for **JACK-O'-LANTERN**, that bright little sprite,

K is for **KELPIE** with the great shining teeth,

L is for **LOCH NESS** and the **MONSTER** beneath,

M is for **MERMAID** who appears from the deep,

N is for **NIGHTMARE** that troubles our sleep,

O is for the **OPERA PHANTOM** who sings,

P is for **PHOENIX** with fiery wings,

Q is for **QUASIMODO** who swings from his bell,

R is for **ROC**, the great bird of Hell,

S is for **SANDMAN**, he'll steal every dream,

T is for **TROLL** 'neath the bridge by the stream,

U is for **UNICORN** with her long horn of gold,

V is for **VAMPIRE** in his tomb dark and cold,

W is for **WEREWOLF** who howls 'neath the sky,

X is for **XANTHUS,** the horse that can fly,

Y is for **YETI**, that abominable beast,

Z is for **ZOMBIE**, the last, but not least.

Tonight's the Night!

'I don't want to go out tonight, Mum,
I don't want to go out tonight.
There's a whistling wind and a cold yellow moon,
And shadows dance eerily out in the gloom,
I'd like to stay home in my own little room,
I don't want to go out tonight.'

'But you must go out tonight, my dear,
It's the night when you have to be seen.
So put on your cloak and pick up the black cat,
Find your spells and your long pointed hat,
And get on your broomstick and fly like a bat,
You're a witch and tonight's Halloween!'

Leviathan

There are salty sea tales,
Of great white whales,
And monsters of the deep.
Of the red-eyed shark,
Which swims in the dark,
And never ever sleeps.
There are octopuses,
The size of buses,
And a clam with a giant jaw,
Gargantuan rays,
Which spend their days,
On the ocean's sandy floor.

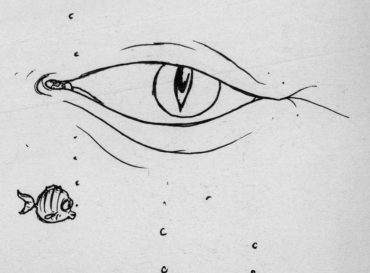

There are mariners' yarns,
Of fish with arms,
And squids that can squeeze you to death.
Of mermaids fair,
With seaweed hair,
That can turn you to stone with their breath.
There are fire-breathing eels,
And two-headed seals,
And a crab with a giant claw,
Pale creatures of jelly,
That lie on their belly,
On the ocean's sandy floor.

But such legends of old,
Don't compare with those told,
Of the greatest sea monster of all.
Its long deadly tail,
Is covered in scales,
And its head is a fiery ball.
The teeth sharp and white,
Have a venomous bite,
And it utters a deafening roar.
The huge eyes they glow,
As it drags you below,
To the ocean's sandy floor.

The Banshee

Bar the door
And bolt the shutter!
No one stir,
Speak or mutter.
Hark! Can you hear it,
Eerily howling
Endlessly prowling?

Nightmare Noises

On a cliff-top perched up high,
Underneath a blood-red sky,
A gloomy grim-walled castle stands.
Its turrets rise like great grey hands,
And windows stare, light sightless eyes,
And echoing round the walls are cries,
Of creatures long since dead.

As the shadows dance and darken,
To the ghostly chorus hearken,
Hear the headless horseman's call,
As he gallops through the hall.
Hear the werewolf's snarling bark,
As he's creeping through the dark,
And baying at the moon.

Mouldering soldiers in armour clank,
In the dungeons cold and dank,
Gruesome gremlins gobble-gabble,
Wicked witches bibble-babble.
Disembodied spirits howl,
And scream and squeal and screech and yowl,
Their haunting symphony.

Mummies from their dusty tomb,
Shuffle in the ghostly gloom,
Monsters grunt and growl and groan,
And grisly ghouls mewl and moan,
Misty spectres whine and wail,
As through the walls they blithely sail,
Phantoms of the night.

But with the morning's sunshine bright,
The shadows melt in pools of light,
And nightmare sounds they fade away,
And in that castle cold and grey,
It's as silent as the grave.

Amphisbaena

You will not find a creature that's meaner
Than the two-headed Amphisbaena.
It has the wings of a bat,
And the claws of a cat,
And a tail like a great concertina.

Monster Alphabet 2

Don't attack an **ALIEN** with an anchor,

Don't bash a **BASILISK** on its brain,

Don't crack **COLOSSUS** with a crowbar,

Don't drag a **DRAGON** down the drain.

Don't entertain **EGOR** in the evening,

Don't frighten **FRANKENSTEIN** when he's in bed

Don't grab a **GREMLIN** in the garden

Don't hit a **HARPY** on the head.

Don't ignore **IGUANODONS** at the ice-rink,

Don't jab a **JABBERWOCKY** on the jaw,

Don't keep a **KRAKEN** in the coal-house,

Don't listen to the **LADON'S** lonely roar.

Don't marry a **MERMAID** in the morning,

Don't knock a **NOKK** on the knee,

Don't offer **OGRES** orange omelettes,

Don't invite a **PHANTOM** home for tea!

Don't question **QUASIMODO** when he's quiet,

Don't rush a **ROBOT** when it rains,

Don't squash the **SANDMAN** when he's sleeping

Don't tie a **TRIFFID** up in chains!

Don't upset a **UNICORN** with an ulcer,

Don't view a **VAMPIRE** with the flu,

Don't wash a **WEREWOLF** in warm water,

Don't X-ray a **YETI** when he's eating cold spaghetti,

Don't zap a **ZOMBIE** at the zoo!

Because if you DO ...
They may just get YOU ...

The Nightmare

I must admit I do not like
My room when Mum turns out the light.
I start to think of scary things:
Of vampire bats with leathery wings,
A werewolf with its fearsome growl,
A wicked witch with scary scowl,
A banshee with its mournful cry,
The cyclops with his one large eye,
A headless ghost which moans and groans,
A skeleton with clacking bones.
But there's one thing I fear the most:
It's not a bat or witch or ghost,
It is the most horrific creature,
It's Mr Wilson, my headteacher!

Note to the Headteacher

I'm a wee bit worried about Wolfgang,
The new boy who's just joined the school.
He's only been here for the morning,
And already has broken every rule.
For a start he wasn't in uniform,
And rushed in the room all in black,
With a fancy bow-tie and silk waistcoat,
And a great flowing cloak down his back.
I asked him to sit at the front desk,
And hang his black cloak near the door.
He refused and said he would rather
Lie flat on his back on the floor.

At break he avoided the playground,
And remarked that the sun was too bright,
So he sat by himself in the storeroom,
Where there wasn't a splinter of light.
After break I gave all the milk out,
But he said it would do him no good,
It was sickly and smelly and tasteless,
And could he have a nice cup of blood!
Then he refused to see the school dentist,
And said his teeth were all fine,
And if anyone doubted this statement,
He'd bite their neck anytime!

When we talked about pets we were fond of,
Most of the children said cats,
And rabbits and hamsters and gerbils,
But he said he'd rather have bats.
He certainly looks quite off-colour,
His face is all pasty and white,
And his dark eyes are staring and bloodshot,
I think he stays up late at night.
He says where he sleeps is quite draughty,
That his bedroom is centuries old,
And it's very cramped up in the coffin,
And dirty and covered in mould.

It could be a question of diet,
Too many sweets, buns and cake,
What he needs is vitamins and proteins,
Maybe a nice piece of steak.
I think we should write to his father,
And say that the school's not equipped,
To deal with a child of his nature,
He'd be better off home in the crypt.
So, you see why I'm worried about Wolfgang,
The new boy who's just joined the school,
And if you want my honest opinion,
I think he's a right little ghoul.

Miss Van Helsing

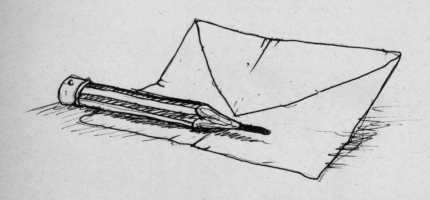

A Dead-End Job

My dad's not a chemist or cabinetmaker,
A butcher or banker, a blacksmith or baker,
A saddler or surgeon, a soldier or sailor,
A tinsmith or typist, a tinker or tailor.

My dad's not a pedlar or plumber or porter,
A docker or dentist, or newspaper reporter,
A physician, policeman, postman or preacher,
A fisherman, farmer, florist or teacher.

My dad's not an engineer or explorer,
A chauffeur or chemist, a locksmith or lawyer,
A jockey or joiner, a judge or a waiter,
A sculptor or shepherd, a singer or slater.

My dad's not a cowboy, a clown or a rector,
An expert on fossils or old architecture,
A caddie, cashier or a refuse collector,
He's out of this world: he's the phantom inspector.

When all of the children are tucked in their beds,
And all the teachers, school cleaners, caretakers and heads,
He visits the schools in the dead of the night,
Where there isn't a sound or a splinter of light.

He floats to the entrance as quiet as you please,
And opens the lock with his skeleton keys.
Then he creeps down the corridors silent as death
And turns the air cold with his wintry breath.

Great ghostly footprints he leaves on the floor
As he walks through the walls and the headteacher's door.
He checks that the classrooms are tidy and clean,
That no litter, graffiti or mess can be seen.

He sees that the books are all marked up to date,
Examines the registers to see who has been late.
In the boiler-house and kitchens he has a quick look,
And writes everything down in his exorcise book.

Then before sunrise when the dark shadows flee,
He locks up the school with his skeleton key,
And he adds the report to the ghostly collection,
And waits for the night and the next school inspection.

My dad's not a steeplejack, salesman or stoker,
A bishop or barrister, barman or broker.
A fruiterer, farrier or football selector,
He's out of this world: he's the phantom inspector.

Six Cinquains

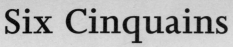

Old house.
Dark and cold.
A musty smell of mould,
And giant shivering shadows,
Waiting.

A light
Under the door,
A whispering inside.
I run back up the stairs in fright.
Phantom!

Beanstalk
Reaches skywards,
Writhes like a giant snake,
And leads to untold riches and …
The Ogre!

Fat troll,
Under the bridge,
Lurking in the darkness.
Hears the trip-trap, trip-trap, trip-trap,
Dinner!

Billy goat
Over the bridge,
Strutting in the sunshine,
Makes the trip-trap, trip-trap, trip-trap,
No fear!

Troll-goat,
Both on the bridge,
Staring at each other.
Each says, 'I want to eat you up!'
Splash! Splash!

The Kraken

Below the cliff,
Below the beach,
Beneath the sea,
Out of reach.
Beside his rock,
Behind the weeds,
Before his cave,
The Kraken feeds!

His eyes are green,
Like emeralds bright,
His beard is long
And black as night.
His face is pale,
His teeth are sharp,
And he sits alone
In the murky dark.

Below the cliff,
Beyond the beach,
Beneath the sea,
Out of reach.
Beside his rock,
Behind the weeds,
Before his cave,
The Kraken feeds!

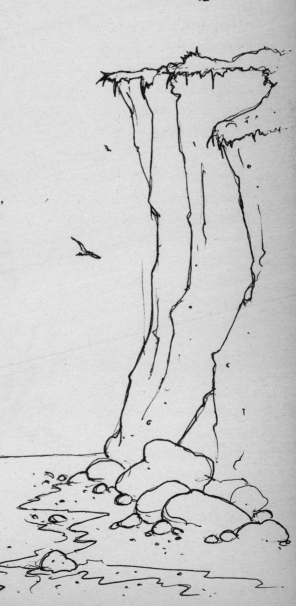

Prawns and shrimps
Are not his meal,
Nor oyster, lobster,
Shark or seal.
He does not care for
Salt sea fish.
The Kraken likes
A tastier dish!

Below the cliff,
Beyond the beach,
Beneath the sea,
Out of reach.
Beside his rock,
Behind the weeds,
Before his cave
The Kraken feeds!

When the storm clouds
Mask the sky,
And mountainous waves
Rise way up high.
When the fierce winds
Shriek and blow,
The Kraken stirs
Deep down below.

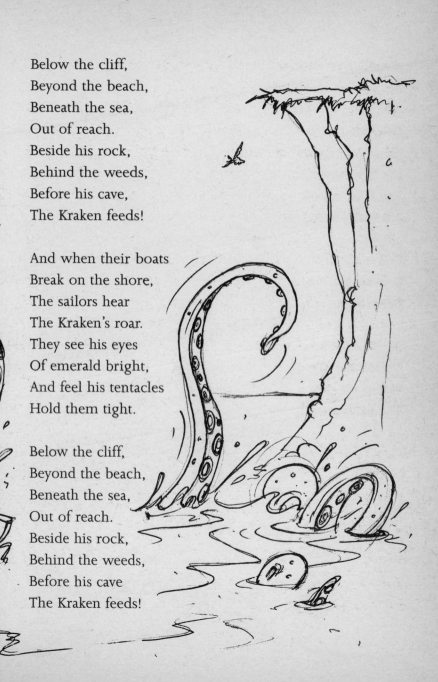

Below the cliff,
Beyond the beach,
Beneath the sea,
Out of reach.
Beside his rock,
Behind the weeds,
Before his cave,
The Kraken feeds!

And when their boats
Break on the shore,
The sailors hear
The Kraken's roar.
They see his eyes
Of emerald bright,
And feel his tentacles
Hold them tight.

Below the cliff,
Beyond the beach,
Beneath the sea,
Out of reach.
Beside his rock,
Behind the weeds,
Before his cave
The Kraken feeds!

Whales and winkles
Are not his meal,
Nor mussel, whelk,
Nor crab or eel.
He does not care
For salt sea fish,
The Kraken eats
A human dish.

Below the cliff,
Beyond the beach,
Beneath the sea,
Out of reach.
Beside his rock,
Behind the weeds,
Before his cave,
The Kraken feeds!

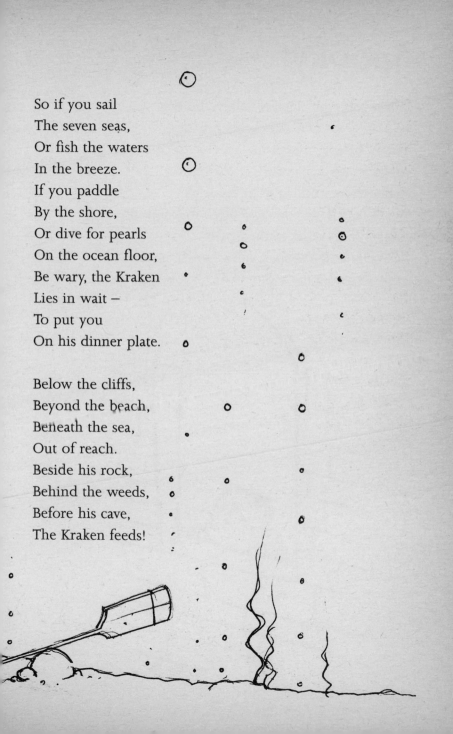

So if you sail
The seven seas,
Or fish the waters
In the breeze.
If you paddle
By the shore,
Or dive for pearls
On the ocean floor,
Be wary, the Kraken
Lies in wait –
To put you
On his dinner plate.

Below the cliffs,
Beyond the beach,
Beneath the sea,
Out of reach.
Beside his rock,
Behind the weeds,
Before his cave,
The Kraken feeds!

Spooky!

When great grey clouds darken the sky,
And the trees look like skeleton hands,
When the cold moon dies,
And stars are like eyes,
And a white mist clings to the land,
When mad dogs howl and black bats squeak,
And fat frogs croak in the gloom,
When lightning flashes, and thunder crashes,
I stay in bed in my room.

A White Wizard's Spell

Take a cauldron the size of the world,

Put in: a handful of happiness,
              a spoonful of smiles,
              a ladleful of laughter,
              and a sprig of honesty.

Mix together well.

Then add: a fistful of fun,
              a gallon of goodness,
              a cup of happiness,
              and a touch of tenderness.

Stir well.

              Sprinkle with a lot of love.

Young Frankenstein

Frankenstein asked his little boy:
'Why are you so sad?
You wander round without a sound,
Come now, tell your dad!'

With grave expression the child replied,
'I'm lonely all the day,
I've lots of toys, like other boys,
But no body with whom to play.'

The Werewolf

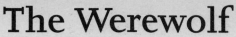

Moon watcher,
Grey growler,
Wood stalker,
Night howler,
Shape changer,
Dark prowler.

The Legend of the Lambton Worm

There's a very famous story
About a serpent and a well –
The story of the Lambton Worm,
A story I will tell.

It happened one fine Monday
In the forest near a lake,
That the Lord of Lambton Castle
Came upon a snake.

It was a tiny wriggly thing
With a rather fishy smell,
So the Lord of Lambton Castle
Dropped it down a nearby well.

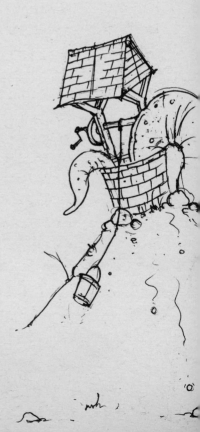

Then he forgot about it
And went fighting far away,
But the worm it grew and grew
To be slimy, fat and grey.

One day it slithered from the well
And, roaring like a leopard,
It swallowed up a flock of sheep,
The sheepdog and the shepherd.

For years and years the creature lived,
Devouring all it saw,
When one day brave Lord Lambton
Came back from the war.

He put his helmet on his head
And with his sword and shield
He climbed up every mountain and
He looked in every field.

Until he found the Lambton Worm
With eyes of fiery red
And he lifted up his great sharp sword
And chopped off the big black head.

Then he cut it into pieces
And he dropped it down the well
And that was the end of the Lambton Worm
So story-tellers tell.

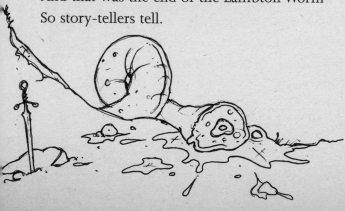

The Ghost Train

The station is no longer used,
The platform's sprouting grass,
The waiting-room's deserted,
And full of broken glass.

The signal box is empty,
The tracks are red with rust,
The Station Master's Office
Is locked and filled with dust.

But at the stroke of midnight,
When all is dark and still,
You might hear a train approaching,
Rumbling up the hill.

You might see the clouds of billowing smoke,
Like phantoms in the night.
You might hear the piercing whistle,
As a dark shape looms in sight.

You might smell the oily engine,
And hear the clickety-clack,
As through the tunnel comes the train,
Travelling up the track.

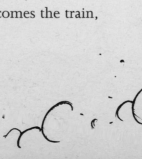

No one knows from where it comes,
Nor where's its destination,
But the air is colder than the grave,
When it pulls into the station.

The engine seems to whisper,
As the coach doors open wide:
'The journey is about to start,
Why don't you step inside?'

Do not listen to the whispers,
Do not clamber on the train,
I'm warning you, those that do
Are never seen again.

So, at the stroke of midnight,
When all is dark and still,
Stay close to home and do not roam
To the station on the hill.

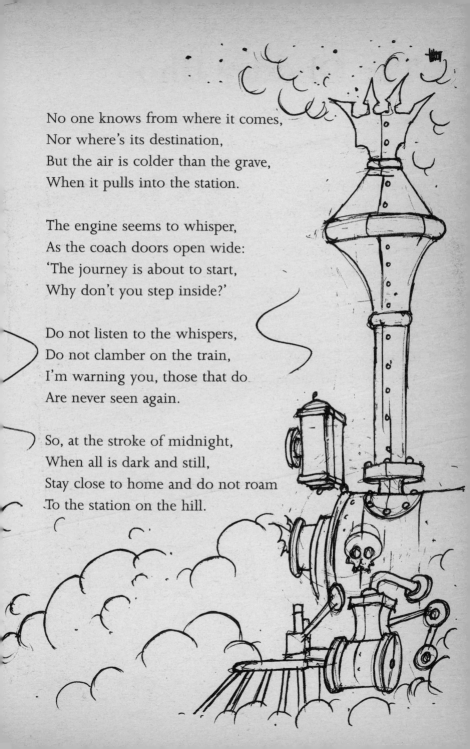

The Moddey Dhoo

The Moddey Dhoo,
The Moddey Dhoo,
You can't see him,
But he sees you.
The Moddey Dhoo,
The Moddey Dhoo,
The phantom hound,
The Moddey Dhoo.

At midnight when the world it sleeps,
Across the moor a creature creeps,
He wanders here, he wanders there,
It's the phantom hound. Beware! Beware!

The Moddey Dhoo,
The Moddey Dhoo,
You can't see him,
But he sees you.
The Moddey Dhoo,
The Moddey Dhoo,
The phantom hound,
The Moddey Dhoo.

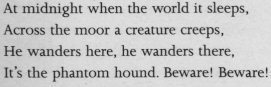

White are his teeth and sharp his claws,
Long are his legs and huge his paws,
Red are his eyes and black his hair.
It's the phantom hound. Beware! Beware!

The Moddey Dhoo,
The Moddey Dhoo,
You can't see him,
But he sees you.
The Moddey Dhoo,
The Moddey Dhoo,
The phantom hound,
The Moddey Dhoo.

Lock the windows, bar the door,
Don't venture out on to the moor,
For he is waiting just for you,
The phantom hound – the Moddey Dhoo

The Moddey Dhoo,
The Moddey Dhoo,
You can't see him,
But he sees you.
The Moddey Dhoo,
The Moddey Dhoo,
The phantom hound,
The Moddey Dhoo.

Nobody's There!

The moon was full that winter's night,
And icy was the air.
I knocked and knocked upon the door,
But nobody was there.

The rooms were deathly silent,
And the walls were cold and bare.
'Hello!' I cried. 'Hello!' again,
But nobody was there.

I thought I heard a floorboard creak,
And whispering on the stair,
But when I turned to greet my host,
Why, nobody was there.

Late that night in bed alone,
I said a silent prayer,
For I felt cold fingers on my cheek,
But nobody was there.

I saw a face, an ashen face,
With white and flowing hair,
But when I blinked and looked again,
Why, nobody was there.

Oh, it was such a mournful face,
Those eyes, how they did stare,
I told myself 'tis but a dream,
That nobody was there.

Now, every night I see that face,
It haunts my dreams – I swear,
But everyone who hears my tale,
They tell me I'm not there.

The Troll

You might have heard this tale before,
When you were five or maybe four,
About the troll who spent all day
Waiting for goats to come his way.
Over the bridge they came *Trip-trap*
Then he'd jump out, *Snip-snap! Snip-snap!*
In one great gulp, he'd eat them whole.
Well – that is how the story's told.
Now this account is just not true,
So, let me here enlighten you.
There *was* a troll, so far so good,
Who lived beneath a bridge of wood,
And animals each day would pass
Across the bridge in search of grass.
But far from being cruel and sly,
The troll was really rather shy.
He never ventured forth by day,
For he knew he'd frighten folk away.
The troll was such a gentle creature,
But had not one redeeming feature.
His back was bent, his legs were long,
His nails were sharp, his arms were strong.
He had the most enormous jaws,
And large flat ears like pointed oars.
With teeth to rival any shark,
And skin as thick and hard as bark

And curved nose like an eagle's beak.
Poor troll, he really looked a freak.
He couldn't help how he appeared,
Great red-rimmed eyes and straggly beard,
So round and squat and strangely hairy,
Extremely ugly and very scary.
So 'neath the bridge he made his home
Where he could hide away alone,
Far from those mean and prying eyes,
The hurtful comments, mocking cries.
But when the world was fast asleep,
From 'neath his wooden bridge he'd creep
And in the still of the silent night,
He'd moonbathe in the silvery light,
And hear the night owl's mournful cry,
And count the stars high in the sky.
At daybreak he would creep away
Under the bridge to spend his day.
In his dark and desolate home,
The troll would slumber there, alone.
Then one day he awoke from sleep.
He heard the timbers groan and creak,
And then a dreadful, deafening rapping
Great thunderous hooves, a trip-trip trapping.
'What is that frightening sound?' he cried.
And through a crack, a goat he spied.
'I thought the world was falling in,
There was the most appalling din.

The noise was such to wake the dead!'
And to the goat, the troll he said:
'I'm trying to have a little nap,
And all I hear is trip-trip trap.
Oh, little goat, please have a care,
When walking on this thoroughfare,
To exercise some moderation,
And please, show some consideration.'
'Go soak your face!' the goat he snapped,
Then louder he trip-trap, trip-trapped.

He skipped and sprang, he jumped and danced,
He hopped and bounced, he leapt and pranced.
The kid made such a hullabaloo,
Poor troll, he didn't know what to do.
The goat, of course, just did not know,
What creature lived there down below.
He had not seen the enormous jaws,
The large flat ears like pointed oars,
The teeth to rival any shark,
And skin as thick and hard as bark,
The red-rimmed eyes and straggly beard.
So when the creature then appeared,
Round and squat and strangely hairy,
Extremely ugly and very scary,
The goat let out a direful scream,
And then fell headlong in the stream.
He splashed and thrashed and bleated madly.
'I'm sorry you fell,' the troll said sadly.
'I did not mean to scare you silly,
Here, let me help you, little billy.'
The goat let out another scream,
Then floated quickly down the stream.
'I'm telling Mum and Dad!' he cried.
'You pushed me in the stream,' he lied.
Now later, when the sun had set,
The troll from 'neath his bridge he crept,
And in the still of the silent night,
He moonbathed in the silvery light,

And heard the night owl's mournful cry,
And counted stars high in the sky.
Then all the peace and quiet was shattered,
Across the bridge some monster clattered.
Trip-trap! Trip-trap! Trip-trap! Trip-trap!
The noise was like a thunderclap.
The beast was of enormous size,
With great sharp horns and flashing eyes,
And hooves of iron and shaggy coat.
It was a giant billy goat.
'Where is that troll,' the goat he screamed,
'Who pushed my son into the stream?
I'll biff him, bash him, butt him silly,
For bullying my little billy.'
The troll cried out, 'Let me explain,'
But all his words were said in vain.
The goat he bellowed, snorted, huffed,
He roared and yelled and stamped and puffed.
Then fast across the bridge he came
As swift as any speeding train.
With lowered horns and eyes a-gleam,
He tipped the troll into the stream.
Now that's the honest truth, my friend,
Of how the poor troll met his end.
So don't believe it if you're told
The troll was big and bad and bold.
And should someone this yarn regale,
They are telling you a fairy-tale.

The Dream Taker

I am the moaning on the breeze,
I am the groaning in the trees,
I am the creaking on the stair,
I am the noise when no one's there.

I am the rattling in the eaves,
I am the rustling in the leaves,
I am the squeaking of the chair,
I am the noise when no one's there.

I am the whispering in the grass,
I am the tapping on the glass,
I am the murmuring in the air,
I am the noise when no one's there.

But when you drift to peaceful sleep,
Into your head I quickly creep,
And there, before the break of day,
I quietly steal your dreams away.

Sleepless Night

There's a boggart in the bathroom,
And a banshee 'neath the bed.
There's a pixie in the pantry,
And a spook without a head.
There's a goblin in the garden,
And a phantom in the hall.
There's an ogre on the landing,
And a sprite behind the wall.
There's a kelpie in the kitchen,
And a ghoul beneath the floor.
There's a fairy on the ceiling,
And an imp behind the door.
There a genie in the attic,
There's a spectre on the stair,
And a wizard in the toilet
With long and flowing hair.

It's no wonder when, at bedtime,
And 'neath the sheets I creep
I haven't a ghost of a ghost of a chance
Of getting off to sleep!

Ghosts

There's a ghost in the garden,
There's a ghost on the stair.
No one can see him
But we all know he's there.

He's a:

Wind whistler,
Floor creaker,
Curtain rustler,
Door squeaker,
Candle flickerer,
Fire crackler,
Shadow mover,
Twig cracker,
Leaf shuffler,
Branch snapper,
Grass whisperer,
Window tapper.

There's a ghost in the garden,
There's a ghost on the stair.
No one can see him
But we all know he's there.

The Bunyip

If you should see a bunyip,
In his wet and weedy bed,
Don't stroke his soft and silvery fur,
Don't pat his hairy head,
Don't tickle him beneath his chin,
Don't look him in the eye.
Just smile and say, 'How do you do,'
And quickly walk on by.

You may think that he's friendly,
You may think that he is mild,
But behind the sighs and gentle eyes
The bunyip is wild.
His teeth are sharp as needles,
And his claws are long and red,
And he waits for little boys and girls,
In his wet and weedy bed.

So, if you should see a bunyip,
Remember what I said.
Don't stroke his soft and silvery fur,
Don't pat his hairy head,
Don't tickle him beneath his chin,
Don't look him in the eye.
Just smile and say, 'How do you do,'
And quickly walk on by.

Glossary

AMPHISBAENA (Greek mythology)
This fearsome, two-headed, dragon-like creature was capable of giving a deadly bite. While one head slept, the other remained awake so it could never be surprised. It could move over the ground at great speed, forwards and backwards, hence the name Amphisbaena, which is the Greek for *goes both ways*. It was slain by St Michael.

BANSHEE (Celtic mythology)
A frightening spirit of Irish and Scottish folklore. In Scotland it was known as the 'Little Washer of Sorrows'. The banshee was a phantom with long flowing hair and pale ghost-like face. She wailed and moaned when someone was about to die.

BASILISK (Roman mythology)
This strange creature, half serpent and half cockerel, was small but deadly. It could kill with a glance and shrivel everything in sight with one poisonous breath.

BOGGART (Northern English mythology)
This mysterious and mischievous sprite of northern England was a furry little elf with a small pointed tail and large pointed ears.

BUNYIP (Aboriginal mythology)
A ferocious furry animal which lives in Australia and inhabits billabongs, deep pools and streams.

CERBERUS (Greek mythology)
This huge three-headed dog, with a serpent's tail, guarded the gates of Hades (Hell). Heracles overpowered Cerberus and dragged him up from the Underworld.

CHIMERA (Greek mythology)
Fire-breathing, three-headed monster.

COLOSSUS (Greek mythology)
A giant. The Colossus of Rhodes was a giant bronze statue, one of the Seven Wonders of the World.

CYCLOPS (Greek mythology)
One of a race of one-eyed giants encountered by Odysseus in the *Odyssey*, the famous epic poem by Homer. The name comes from the Greek word *kuklops* meaning *round eye*. The most famous Cyclops of all was Polyphemus.

DRAGON
The most famous and possibly the oldest of the Fabulous Beasts, the dragon is found in many cultures throughout the world. The word *drakon* or *draco* was used in Ancient Greece and Rome to describe a large snake. The dragon emerges from an egg lying at the bottom of the sea and is usually slain by a heroic knight. It has been depicted in many different forms but is most often shown with a red, scaly, armour-plated body, large pointed wings, a long and twisting tail and a fiery breath.

EGOR

The man-servant of Baron Frankenstein (see below).

FRANKENSTEIN'S MONSTER

In Mary Shelley's novel, *Frankenstein*, Baron Frankenstein made a monster from dead bodies which he stole from graveyards and morgues, and brought the huge creature to life by an electric current. The monster wanted sympathy but was feared and attacked, and so became a killer.

GHOUL
An evil demon who steals children. The name comes from the Arabic word *ghala* meaning *seized*.

GOBLIN
A small grotesque supernatural creature who gets up to mischief.

GREMLIN
An mischievous imp jokingly said to be responsible for mechanical troubles in equipment.

GRENDEL (Norse legend)
The terrible man-eating, swamp-dwelling monster killed by Beowulf.

GRIFFON or GRIFFIN
A very ancient Fabulous Beast with the foreparts, wings and head of an eagle, the rear, tail and hindlegs of a lion. Feathers grew upon its head, neck and chest but the rest of its body was fur-covered. The griffons were said to be the guardians of great treasures and were fearsome and greedy creatures.

90

HARPIES (Greek mythology)

Frightening birds with human faces known as 'the Ministers of an Untimely Death'.

HYDRA (Greek mythology)

A monster with nine heads, each of which when struck off was replaced by two new ones.

IGUANADON

This was a large dinosaur with a broad stiff tail and a spike on each thumb. The name derives from *iguana* and the Greek *odous odontus* meaning *tooth*.

JABBERWOCKY

This monstrous invention of the writer Lewis Carroll appears in the poem *Jabberwocky*. It has 'jaws that bite', 'claws that catch' and 'eyes of flame'.

KELPIE (Scottish folklore)

A water spirit in the form of a horse that drowned its riders.

KRAKEN (Norse mythology)

This ancient creature is one of the most celebrated of the marine monsters and was said to live deep down in the ocean off the shores of Scandanavia. The name derives from the crustacean crab. It had a smooth round body that was one and a half miles in circumference with many poisonous tentacles attached. It resembled a massive octopus and was sometimes mistaken by sailors for an island.

LADON (Greek mythology)

This was a hundred-headed snake, the offspring of Typhon and Echidna. It helped the Hesperides or nymphs guard the golden apples.

LEPRECHAUNS (Irish mythology)

A tribe of Irish fairy elves less than two feet tall. They haunted wine cellars and guarded an immense treasure. If caught, which was very rarely, they had to take their captor to their 'crock of gold'.

LEVIATHAN (Biblical)

This was the great fish of the Abyss killed by St Gabriel which had as many eyes as there are days in the year. In the Book of Job, Chapter 21, it is described as a vast marine creature with 'eyes like the lids of the morning'. It is said that 'out of his mouth go burning lamps' and 'sparks of fire leap out of his nostrils'.

LOCH NESS MONSTER (Scottish mythology)

A large prehistoric creature with a long neck which lived (or lives) deep in Loch Ness in Scotland. Many think it is a dinosaur.

MEDUSA (Greek mythology)

One of three Gorgons, whose terrible eyes turned anyone to stone who looked into her face. Medusa's hair was entwined with poisonous serpents and her body was covered in hard shiny scales. Perseus killed this monster by looking at her reflection in his shield, so he did not have to gaze into her deadly eyes, and then chopping off her head.

MERMAID (Anglo-Saxon mythology)

A beautiful woman from the waist up and a gleaming fish below, her mournful voice enchanted all who heard it. Some mermaids lured seamen to their doom on reefs and dangerous rocks, others rescued shipwrecked mariners and cared for them, but they would never let them go. The name mermaid comes from the Anglo-Saxon word mer which means sea.

MINOTAUR (Greek mythology)

Half man and half bull, this monster was kept by King Minos of Crete inside the Labyrinth from which no one could escape. Theseus killed the Minotaur.

MODDEY DHOO (Isle of Manx mythology)

There are many legends about the Black Dogs. These include the Barguest, Padfoot, Shrike, Ce Sitt (a dog the size of a calf with a dark-green coat which haunts the highlands of Scotland), and the Moddey Dhoo, the famous Black Dog of Peel which inhabits the Isle of Man. These huge, shaggy-coated beasts with brilliant, fiery red eyes and great white teeth roamed the moors at night looking for their prey. Their wailing howl was advance warning of death.

NOKK (Norse mythology)

A hideous, flesh-eating, human-like creature from Scandinavia, it had long arms and webbed feet and lived in fjords waiting for unwary swimmers and paddlers.

NUCKELAVEE (Scottish mythology)

Celtic monster, half man and half horse, with a barrel-shaped body, a huge head and a pig's snout. It has no skin so its yellow veins can be seen quite clearly. Its breath is poisonous and can wither plants. The only way to escape the Nuckelavee is to cross running water, which the creature cannot abide, or lull it to sleep with beautiful music.

OGRE (Roman mythology)

A man-eating giant. The name comes from the Latin word *Orcus*, the god of the infernal regions.

PEGASUS (Greek mythology)

Winged horse of the Muses which sprang from the blood of Medusa when she had been slain by Perseus.

PHOENIX (Greek mythology)

Fabulous bird the size of an eagle with brilliant-coloured red, gold and blue plumage. When ready to die it built a nest, the sun ignited it, and a new Phoenix rose from the ashes.

POLTERGEIST

Mischievous spirit.

QUASIMODO

Poor, deformed and simple-minded character who rang the bells in the great cathedral of Notre Dame. He appears in the classic novel by Victor Hugo, *Notre Dame de Paris*, and is described as having 'a tetrahedron nose, horse-shoe mouth, small left eye over-shadowed by a red bushy brow, straggling teeth, horny lip and forked chin'.

ROC

An immense eagle so large it could carry an elephant in its claws. Its feathers were as big as palm trees. Sinbad, hero of the *Arabian Nights*, found a Roc's egg as large as 148 hens' eggs. When the adult returned to the nest Sinbad tied himself to the bird's leg and flew with it up into the sky so high he lost sight of the Earth. Eventually Sinbad was able to escape when the Roc landed on another island.

SANDMAN

A magical person supposed to put children to sleep by sprinkling sand in their eyes.

SIRENS (Greek mythology)

Half women, half vulture, these sea nymphs charmed sailors with their beautiful singing before killing them.

SPHINX (Greek mythology)

A monster with the winged body of a lion, renowned for posing unanswerable riddles. Travellers who could not answer her riddle would be eaten up.

SPRITE

A nimble elf-like creature, quite harmless and very shy, who lives by water. The name comes from the Latin word *spiritus* meaning *spirit*.

TRIFFID

Huge, man-eating plant.

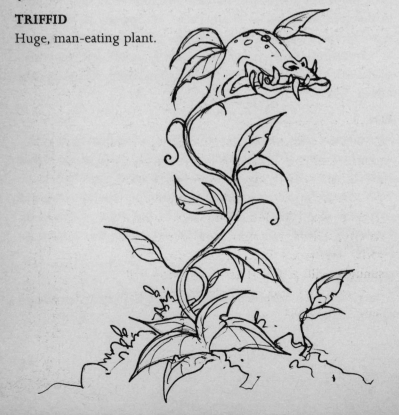

TROLL (Norse mythology)

Originally huge and ugly giants of Scandinavia who could bewitch men. The sound of church bells frightened them away. Night trolls shun the daylight. If they set foot in the light they turn to stone.

UNICORN

One of the most ancient of mythological beasts, this pure white horse with a single horn projecting from its forehead was a shy, gentle and elusive creature. It was hunted for its horn which has magical properties.

VAMPIRE (Eastern European mythology)

Vampires are blood-drinking creatures which could change from human form into bats. The most notorious was Count Dracula, who appears in the novel by Bram Stoker. He lived in the crypt of a ruined castle in Transylvania and lured unsuspecting travellers to their deaths. During the day he slept in a coffin but when the sun had set, he transformed into a bat and went in search of blood. Dracula is finally destroyed by Professor Van Helsing, who, as the monster slept, hammered a stake through his heart. Vampires have no reflection, cannot stand the smell of garlic and recoil from the crucifix. Bright sunlight will shrivel them, holy water will burn them and they can only be killed by a stake to the heart.

WEREWOLF (Eastern European mythology)

The legend of the werewolf tells that at the full moon a man could change into a savage, wolf-like creature. His body and the palms of his hands became covered in fur, his eyes reddened and glowed, claws replaced his nails and his teeth grew to enormous fangs. A bite from a werewolf would turn its victim into another werewolf. It could only be killed by a silver bullet made from a crucifix.

WORM (Anglo-Saxon mythology)

A dragon-like snake with wings or legs, it was immensely long, venomous and slimy. The word *worm* comes from the Norse word *ormr* meaning *dragon*. It inhabited damp or wet places like wells, rivers or lakes. 'The Lambton Worm' is perhaps the most famous but there are others, such as 'The Laidly Worm' and 'The Wode Worm of Linton'.

XANTHUS (Greek mythology)

Xanthus and Balius were the immortal horses of Achilles, offspring of a harpy. They had the power of speech and warned Achilles of his impending death.

YETI (Tibetan mythology)

Also known as 'the Abominable Snowman', the Yeti was a huge bear-like creature covered in long white hair, said to inhabit the Himalayas. Climbers have claimed to have found its large footprints in the snow.

ZOMBIE (Caribbean folklore)

A corpse which is brought to life by magical means. In the West Indies the Zombie is the snake god of the Voodoo cults; in West Africa he is the python god. The name comes from the Kongo word *zumbi* meaning *good-luck fetish*.

Kinds of Poem

ACROSTIC
A poem where the first letter of each line forms a word.

ALPHABET POEM
Where the alphabet is used to give a pattern and structure to the verse.

BALLAD
A narrative poem with a regular rhyme scheme and pounding rhythm which usually deals with fairly violent events. The word *ballad* comes from the Latin *ballare*, meaning *to dance*, and the earliest ballads were intended to accompany music and dance.

FREE VERSE
A poem without rhyme but with rhythm.

HAIKU
Traditionally a Japanese verse form, usually written in seventeen syllables and following the fixed pattern of:
a first line of five syllables,
a second line of seven syllables,
a third line of five syllables.

KENNING
Originally this was an Old Norse or Old English poem where a metaphorical name is used for something, for example *bone house* for *body*. The name comes from the Old Norse word *kenna* meaning *to know*.

LIMERICK
A short, amusing and witty verse of five lines which follows a fixed pattern:

the first, second and fifth lines rhyme,
the third and fourth lines rhyme,
the first, second and fifth lines have three beats,
the third and fourth lines have two beats.

RHYMING POEMS

Full rhyme or ordinary rhyme consists of two words or final syllables of words which sound exactly alike. The couplet has two lines, the quatrain four and the cinquain five.

RIDDLE

A word puzzle. Riddles can be of one line or long and detailed. Some are easy to solve, others very difficult; some are 900 years old, others very modern; some rhyme, others don't.

Index of First Lines

Solutions to Haiku Riddles

1. Sphinx
2. Phoenix
3. Gorgon
4. Pegasus
5. Sirens
6. Harpies
7. Minotaur
8. Cerberus

Read more in Puffin

For complete information about books available from Puffin – and Penguin – and how to order them, contact us at the appropriate address below. Please note that for copyright reasons the selection of books varies from country to country.

www.puffin.co.uk

In the United Kingdom: Please write to Dept EP, Penguin Books Ltd.
Bath Road, Harmondsworth, West Drayton, Middlesex UB7 0DA

In the United States: Please write to Penguin Putnam Inc., P.O. Box 12289,
Dept B, Newark. New Jersey 07101-5289 or call 1-800-788-6262

In Canada: Please write to Penguin Books Canada Ltd,
10 Alcorn Avenue, Suite 300, Toronto, Ontario M4V 3B2

In Australia: Please write to Penguin Books Australia Ltd,
250 Camberwell Road, Camberwell, Victoria 3124

In New Zealand: Please write to Penguin Books (NZ) Ltd,
Private Bag 102902, North Shore Mail Centre, Auckland 10

In India: Please write to Penguin Books India Pvt Ltd,
11 Panscheel Shopping Centre, Panscheel Park. New Delhi 110 017

In the Netherlands: Please write to Penguin Books Netherlands bv,
Postbus 3507, NL-1001 AH Amsterdam

In Germany: Please write to Penguin Books Deutschland GmbH,
Metzlerstrasse 26, 60594 Frankfurt am Main

In Spain: Please write to Penguin Books S. A., Bravo Murillo 19,
1° B, 28015 Madrid

In Italy: Please write to Penguin Italia s.r.l.,
Via Felice Casati 20, I-20124 Milano

In France: Please write to Penguin France S. A.,
17 rue Lejeune, F-31000 Toulouse

In Japan: Please write to Penguin Books Japan, Ishikiribashi Building,
2-5-4, Suido, Bunkyo-ku, Tokyo 112

rica (Pty) Ltd,

3 8002 01144 3498